THE HUMAN BODY IN FOCUS

HOW THE HEART WORKS

KATIE WALLACE

Adapted from an original text by Carol Ballard

W
FRANKLIN WATTS
LONDON•SYDNEY

First published in 2009 by Franklin Watts

Franklin Watts
338 Euston Road
London NW1 3BH

Franklin Watts Australia
Level 17/207 Kent Street, Sydney, NSW 2000

Produced by Arcturus Publishing Limited,
26/27 Bickels Yard, 151–153 Bermondsey Street, London SE1 3HA

Understanding the Human Body is based on the series Exploring the Human Body, published by Franklin Watts.

Editor: Alex Woolf
Designer: Peta Phipps and Mike Reynolds
Illustrator: Michael Courtney
Picture researcher: Glass Onion Pictures
Consultant: Dr Kristina Routh

Picture Credits
Science Photo Library: 5 (Scott Camazine, Sue Trainor), 7 (Zephyr), 11 (Mauro Fermariello), 13 (Susan Kuklin), 15 (Ouellette & Theroux, Publiphoto Diffusion), 16 (Martin Riedl), 17 (Zephyr), 18 (Zephyr), 19 (James King-Holmes), 21 (Mark Clarke), 22 (David Scharf), 24 (Antonia Reeve), 25 (Sam Ogden), 26 (Antonia Reeve), 27 (Tek Image), 28 (Dr Gopal Murti), 29 (Alex Bartel).
Shutterstock: cover (Ken Inness)

A CIP catalogue record for this book is available from the British Library.

Dewey Decimal Classification Number: 612.1'7

ISBN 978 0 7496 9055 7

Printed in China

Franklin Watts is a division of Hachette Children's Books, an Hachette UK Company
www.hachette.co.uk

Contents

Your Amazing **Heart**

Your heart is amazing. From the moment you are born, for your whole life, it never stops beating. You do not even have to think about it. Your heart beats automatically.

Super pump

Your heart sits inside your chest. It is a strong muscle that works like a pump. Every time it beats, it pushes blood around your body. The blood flows through a network of tubes called blood vessels. One network of vessels links the heart to the lungs. Another links the heart to the rest of the body.

One-way system

There are different types and sizes of blood vessel. These all work together like a road network. Blood always flows through the vessels in the same direction. The blood vessels carry blood from the heart to the rest of your body and back to the heart again. This endless journey is called blood **circulation**.

This picture shows the network of blood vessels in the body.

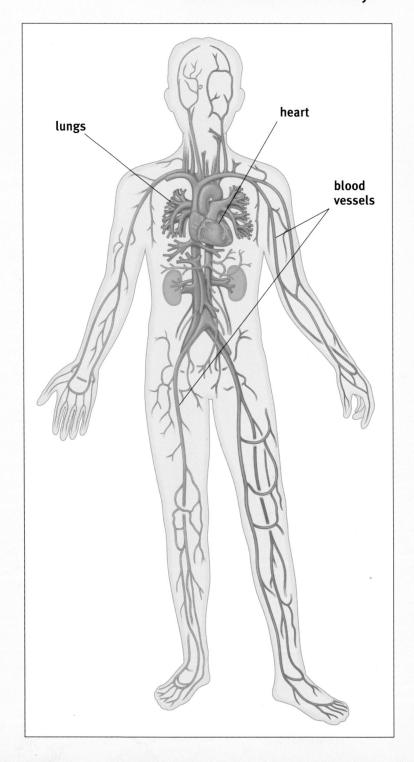

lungs

heart

blood vessels

A healthy heart

Sometimes your heart may beat faster or slower than at other times. This depends on how hard the rest of your body is working. It is important to look after your heart. Regular exercise and a healthy diet help to keep the heart healthy and strong.

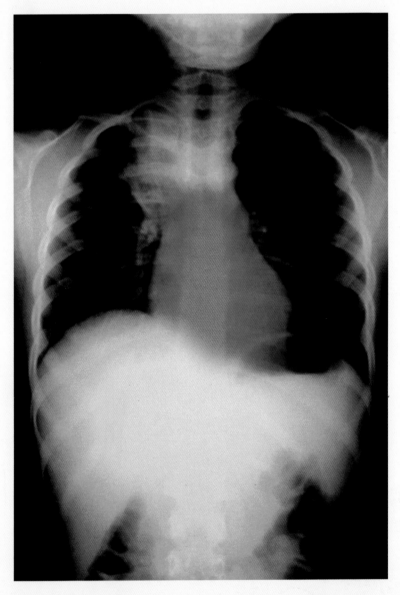

This X-ray shows the heart protected by the ribcage and surrounded by the lungs.

Q&A

Why does blood circulate?

Blood does several important jobs. It carries **oxygen** and food around your body. It defends your body from **germs**. Blood helps to control your body's temperature. It also controls the amounts of water and chemicals in your body. Blood can only do these jobs by circulating to reach every part of your body.

Blood Circulation

Blood flows to every part of your body through a network of tubes called blood vessels. There are blood vessels in every living part of your body. Blood has several important jobs – transport, control and defence.

This diagram shows the two networks of blood vessels as if you are looking in a mirror.

Transporting gases

There are two networks of blood vessels. One carries blood from the right side of your heart to your lungs. As you breathe in, your lungs fill up with air. **Oxygen** from the air moves into the blood and the blood vessels then carry the oxygen-rich blood to the left side of the heart.

Never-ending cycle

The other network of blood vessels carries the oxygen-rich blood from the left side of your heart to the rest of your body. As the blood passes through your organs and muscles, it supplies them with oxygen. The organs and muscles produce a waste gas called **carbon dioxide**. The carbon dioxide is carried in the blood back to the right side of the heart and on to the lungs. Then the cycle begins all over again.

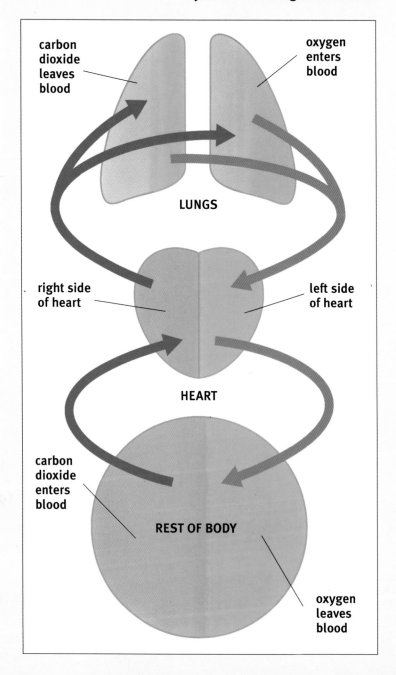

carbon dioxide leaves blood

oxygen enters blood

LUNGS

right side of heart

left side of heart

HEART

carbon dioxide enters blood

REST OF BODY

oxygen leaves blood

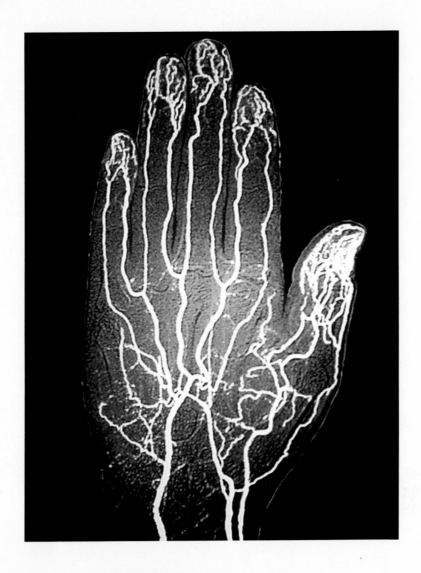

This X-ray shows the blood vessels in a hand.

Blood superhighway

Blood transports other things around your body, too. **Nutrients** from food are carried from your **digestive system** to organs and muscles that need them. Waste chemicals and excess water are taken to the **liver** and **kidneys** to be removed from the blood. As it circulates, your blood also helps to defend your body from **germs**.

Q&A

How long are my blood vessels?

If the blood vessels from an average adult were laid end to end, they would stretch nearly 100,000 kilometres. That's more than twice the distance around the world!

The **Heart**

The heart is a strong, muscular organ. It beats continuously, day and night. It contracts and relaxes to pump blood around your body.

The heart's blood vessels

Your heart needs a regular supply of **oxygen** and **nutrients**. Waste products made by the heart muscle must also be removed. Your heart has its own special blood vessels called the **coronary arteries** and **veins**. These vessels carry oxygen to the heart and carry away its waste.

Other large blood vessels are connected to the heart. The **pulmonary** vein carries blood from the heart to the lungs. The pulmonary artery carries blood from the lungs back to the heart. The **aorta** carries blood from the heart to the body. The **venae cavae** carry blood from the body back to the heart.

Cardiac muscle

Your heart is made up of **cardiac** muscle. Cardiac

Your heart is roughly the same size and shape as your fist.

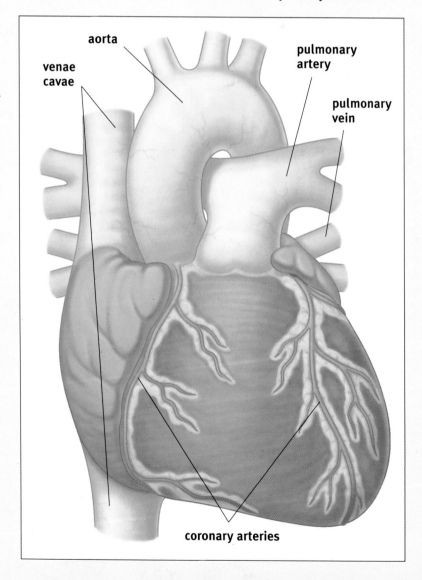

aorta

venae cavae

pulmonary artery

pulmonary vein

coronary arteries

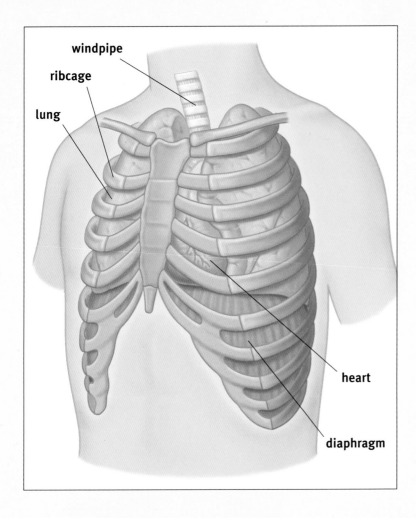

windpipe

ribcage

lung

heart

diaphragm

The heart lies inside the chest. It is protected by the bones of the ribcage.

muscle is different from other muscles in your body. A damaged leg muscle will heal and make new muscle tissue. Damaged cardiac muscle only forms scar tissue. Cardiac muscle can partly control when it contracts. Other muscles only contract when given a signal from the brain.

The pericardium

The heart has a protective outer layer called the **pericardium**. Strong fibres attach the pericardium to the **diaphragm** and the breastbone to hold your heart in place. The pericardium produces a fluid that allows the heart to move smoothly.

Q&A

How big is my heart?

Your heart weighs about 200 grams – about the same as a large potato. As your body grows, so does your heart.

Inside your Heart

Inside your heart are four spaces, called chambers. The top chambers are called **atria**. The bottom chambers are called **ventricles**. A strong wall called the **septum** separates the chambers on the right from those on the left. This prevents blood from each side from mixing. The right side pumps blood to the lungs. The left side pumps blood to the rest of the body.

Valves

Blood flows through the heart in one direction. Strong flaps called **valves** open to let blood flow through them. They snap shut to stop the blood flowing back. When a valve opens, blood flows into the heart. The valve shuts when there is enough blood. Another valve opens to let the blood out. The first valve

This diagram shows the chambers and valves of the heart.

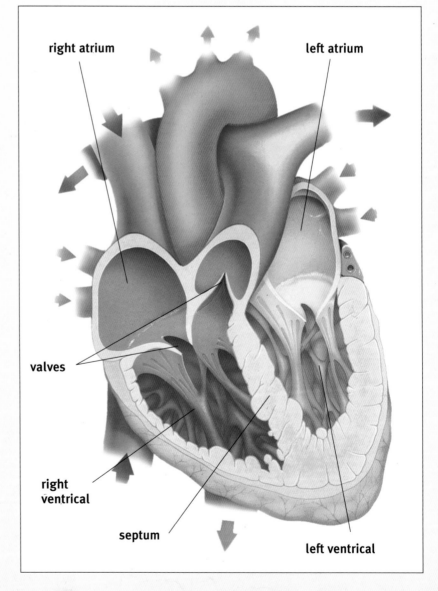

right atrium

left atrium

valves

right ventrical

septum

left ventrical

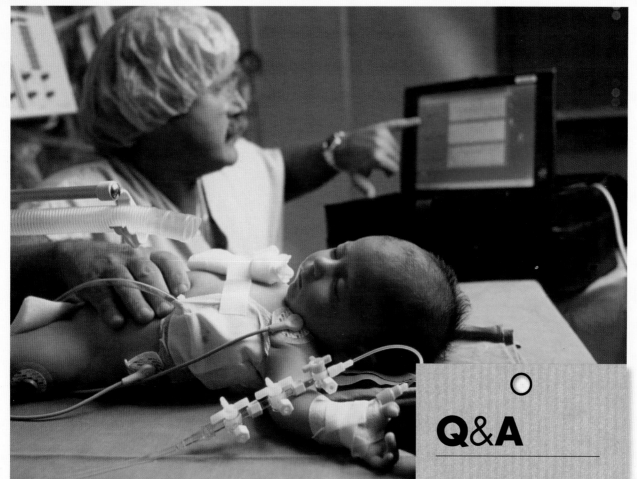

This baby is recovering after heart surgery.

opens again to let in more blood. This provides the heart with the just right amount of blood.

Valve problems
Some people have valves that do not close properly. They may have been faulty at birth, or damaged after an illness. This means that some blood can flow backwards into the heart, so it works less efficiently. Doctors can replace damaged or faulty valves with new ones made of metal or plastic.

Q&A

What is a 'hole in the heart'?
The septum is a wall that stops blood moving from one side of the heart to the other. Some babies are born with a small gap between the two sides, called a 'hole in the heart'. Blood can spill through, making the baby very ill. Doctors can operate to close the hole.

Heart Beat

If you listen to your heartbeat, you can hear the sounds of the **valves** as they snap shut. Each heartbeat has two sounds – lub-dup ... lub-dup ... lub-dup. These are the two pairs of valves shutting one after the other.

Heartbeat stages

There are four stages to every heartbeat.

1. The **atria** fill with blood.
2. The atria contract (squeeze). Blood is forced through the valves, pushing them open. This allows blood to flow into the **ventricles**.
3. When the ventricles are full they contract. The valves between the atria and ventricles close to stop blood flowing backwards. This makes the first sound of the heartbeat ('lub'). The blood forces the next set of valves open. Blood rushes into the blood vessels.
4. The second set of valves shut. This stops the blood flowing back into the ventricles. This makes the second sound of the heartbeat ('dup').

This diagram shows the stages of a single heartbeat.

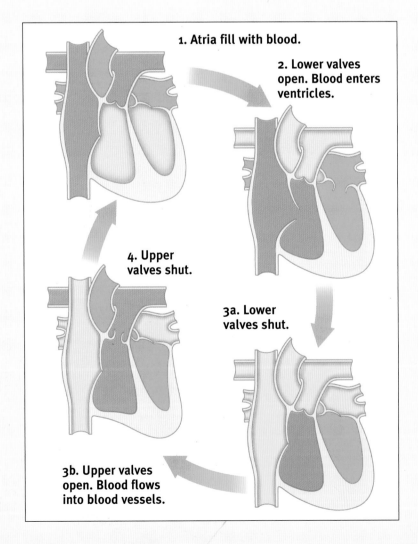

1. Atria fill with blood.

2. Lower valves open. Blood enters ventricles.

3a. Lower valves shut.

3b. Upper valves open. Blood flows into blood vessels.

4. Upper valves shut.

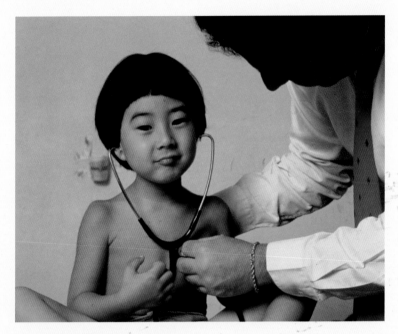

A stethoscope allows you to hear the sound of your heartbeat more clearly.

The big push

The atria immediately fill with blood as soon as the ventricles empty. The ventricle walls are thicker and stronger than those of the atria. This is because the atria need only a gentle push to pump blood into the ventricles. The ventricles need a much stronger push to pump blood into the blood vessels.

Monitoring heartbeats

Doctors use an instrument called a stethoscope to hear how well a patient's heart is working. For a more detailed picture, a doctor may use an electrocardiograph (ECG) machine. This records electrical signals from the heart as it is beating.

Q&A

How do I feel my pulse?

Lay the index and middle finger of one hand gently on your other wrist. You might be able to feel a beat. This is your pulse. It is caused by the heart pumping blood along the **arteries**.

Exercise and Heart Rate

An adults' heart beats roughly 70 or 80 times a minute when they are resting. Some people's hearts beat more quickly than other's. Children usually have a faster heartbeat than this.

Speeding up ...

Your heart beats all the time. If it beats 70 times a minute, that's more than 100,000 beats every day! If you exercise, it will be even more! While exercising, your muscles need more **oxygen** and more energy than when they are resting. They also produce waste more quickly. Your heart has to pump faster so the blood can carry more oxygen and **nutrients** to the muscles, and remove waste products more quickly.

During exercise your heart rate speeds up. After exercise it gradually returns to its normal speed.

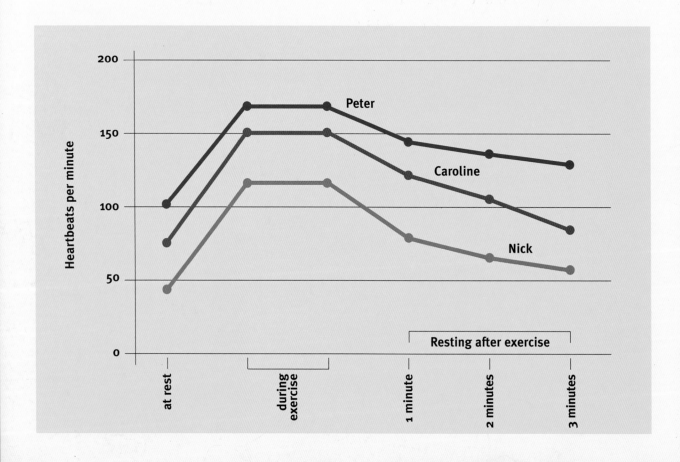

14

Regular exercise keeps
the heart fit and strong.

... Slowing down

After exercise, your muscles need less oxygen
and energy. They also produce less waste. The
blood does not need to be pumped as quickly.
Your heart rate gradually slows down and
returns to normal.

A healthy heart

Regular exercise makes your heart muscle
stronger. It can pump more blood with each
beat. It does not need to increase its rate very
much when you exercise. It also goes back to
normal quickly after exercising.

Q&A

How are heart rate and breathing rate linked?

When you exercise, your
muscles need more
oxygen. You need to
breathe more quickly and
deeply. Your heart has to
pump more quickly to carry
the oxygen to your
muscles and remove the
waste **carbon dioxide**.
When you rest, you need
less oxygen, so your
breathing rate slows down.

Healthy Heart

If you look after your heart, it will look after you!
You can do several things to keep your heart fit
and healthy.

Get sporty

Regular exercise makes your heart fitter and
stronger – and it's fun, too. Dancing, swimming,
cycling and team games will all help your heart
stay strong. Many doctors recommend that you
exercise at least four or five times a week.

**Swimming is fantastic
for your heart!**

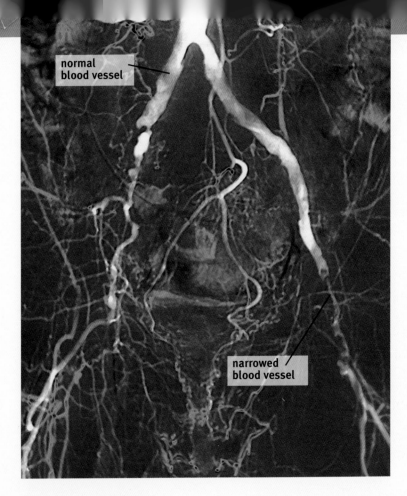

normal
blood vessel

narrowed
blood vessel

This X-ray shows damaged blood vessels. Blood struggles to get through the narrow sections.

Healthy eating

A balanced diet keeps your heart and body healthy. Eat something from each of these groups of foods every day and you will be bursting with energy:

- fresh fruit and vegetables – for vitamins and minerals
- wholemeal bread, pasta, rice or other cereals – for energy
- meat, fish, eggs and nuts – for protein.

Avoid eating too many sugary and fatty foods. They are fine once in a while but they do not give your body the **nutrients** it needs.

No smoking!

Cigarettes are bad news for your heart. Some chemicals in cigarette smoke make your blood vessels narrower. Your heart then has to work harder to push the blood through them. This extra strain can damage the heart and lead to heart disease.

Q&A

Does being overweight affect my heart?

Being very overweight puts greater strain on your heart. Overweight people often have higher blood pressure. This means the heart has to work harder to push blood around the body. Also, the heart has to pump blood to the extra fat tissue. This makes it harder for the heart to work properly and eventually damages it.

Heart Attacks

A blockage in the **coronary** blood vessels may cause a heart attack. Blood cannot reach part of the heart muscle. Without fresh blood, this part of the heart dies. This stops the heart beating properly. The patient may die without medical help.

Warning signs

For men, the first sign of a heart attack is a severe chest pain. Women may feel sick and very tired. The patient's left hand and arm may tingle. They may find it hard to breathe.

Expert help

Medical teams have to act quickly to prevent further damage to the heart. Medicines can help to remove the blockage in the coronary vessels. If the heart has stopped beating, the heart is given an electric shock to make it beat again. Mouth-to-mouth resuscitation and chest massage may help to keep blood flowing through the body until the heart beats normally.

After a heart attack, doctors carry out tests reveal any damage to the heart.

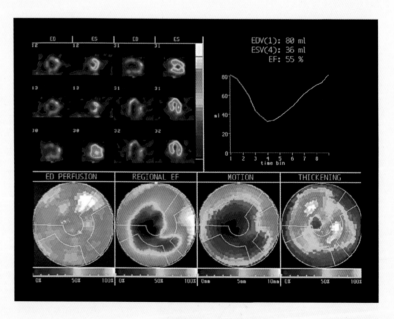

This screen shows the results of heart tests after a heart attack.

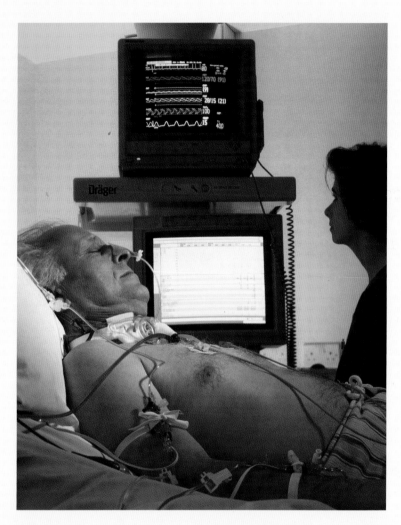

This heart-attack patient is being monitored in hospital.

Patients are also advised to eat a low-fat diet, exercise regularly and not smoke cigarettes.

Who is at risk?

Heart attacks are more common in smokers, overweight people and people who eat fatty diets. People with very stressful lives are also at risk. Some medical conditions, such as diabetes, can increase the risk of a heart attack. Heart attacks may be more common in some families than in others.

Q&A

What should I do in an emergency?

If you think someone is having a heart attack, keep calm. If there is an adult nearby, ask for help. If not, find a telephone and dial 999. Tell the operator who you are and what the problem is. Answer any questions they ask and follow their instructions.

Blood Vessels

There are three main types of blood vessel: **arteries**, **veins** and **capillaries**. Each type has a different job to do.

Arteries

Arteries carry blood away from the heart. When the heart beats, blood rushes into the arteries under high pressure. Arteries have strong, muscular walls to cope with this pressure. Artery walls have a thick outer layer, a middle layer of muscles and fibres, and a thin lining layer.

Veins

Veins carry blood back to the heart. Their walls do not need to be as strong as artery walls because the blood is under less pressure. The outer and inner layers of vein walls are similar to those of arteries. The middle layer is thinner and has fewer muscles. Veins have **valves** that stop your blood from flowing backwards.

Capillaries

Capillaries link arteries and veins together. Arteries branch into

These diagrams show the different structures of arteries, veins and capillaries.

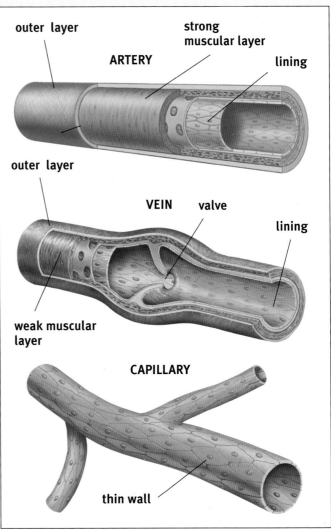

outer layer

strong muscular layer

ARTERY

lining

outer layer

VEIN   valve

lining

weak muscular layer

CAPILLARY

thin wall

narrower and narrower tubes. Eventually they branch into the narrowest blood vessels, or capillaries. The capillaries carry blood through the body tissues.

Capillary walls are so thin that gases and chemicals can pass through them. **Nutrients** and **oxygen** pass from the blood in the capillaries into the body tissues. Waste products pass from the body tissues into the capillaries. These are carried away by the blood.

Some capillaries lie just beneath your skin. When you are hot, more blood flows through these capillaries. This helps you lose heat through your skin. When you are cold, less blood flows through these capillaries. This keeps heat inside your body.

Blood flowing through this boy's skin capillaries helps to cool him down.

Q&A

What are varicose veins?

Varicose veins look like dark, lumpy lines under the skin. Weak valves in the veins allow blood to flow backwards, stretching and twisting the veins. Pregnant women and people who have to stand for long periods often get varicose veins. In serious cases an operation can remove them.

Blood

Blood is your body's transport system. It defends your body against **germs**. Blood helps to control the amounts of water and chemicals in your body. It also helps to control your body's temperature. But what is blood made of?

Each drop of blood contains millions and millions of red blood cells.

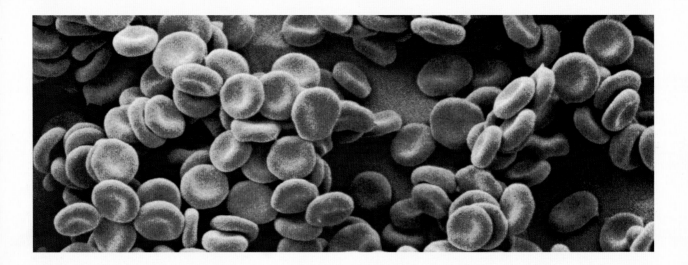

Blood cells

There are several different types of blood cell:

Red blood cells are tiny discs that carry **oxygen** around your body. They give your blood its red colour.

White blood cells are your body's defence system. Some produce chemicals to destroy germs. Others surround harmful particles and destroy them.

Platelets are tiny pieces of cells. They help your blood to clot and form a scab.

Plasma

Blood cells float around in a clear liquid called **plasma**. Plasma carries chemicals and **nutrients** to every part of your body. It transports waste chemicals to the **liver** or **kidneys** to be removed.

Making blood cells

Blood cells are made in your bone marrow, a soft material at the centre of some bones. Some white blood cells only live for a day or two. Others may live for a few months. Red blood cells live for about three months. Worn-out blood cells are destroyed by your spleen and liver. The chemicals they were made from are stored, reused or removed by your urine.

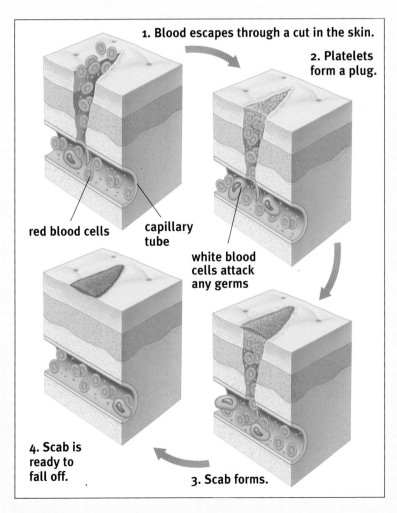

1. Blood escapes through a cut in the skin.

2. Platelets form a plug.

red blood cells

capillary tube

white blood cells attack any germs

4. Scab is ready to fall off.

3. Scab forms.

This diagram shows how a scab forms.

Q&A

What happens when I cut myself?

After a small cut, blood oozes from the wound. The blood soon stops flowing from your skin. **Platelets** in your blood contain chemicals to make the blood stick together, or clot. They make a mesh over the cut and form a scab. The cut heals underneath, forming new skin. When the cut is healed, the scab falls off.

Blood Groups

All humans have **red blood cells**, but the cells may have different chemicals on their surfaces. Scientists look at these chemicals to put blood into different groups.

The ABO system

The main blood group system is called ABO. The ABO system looks for two chemicals, A and B, which may be found on your red blood cells. These chemicals determine your ABO blood group. The table below shows how this works:

A scientist tests some blood to see which group it belongs to.

Blood group	Chemical on blood cells
A	A
B	B
AB	A and B
O	neither A nor B

Blood from different groups should not be mixed together. They may react against each other and make you very ill. If you need an operation, doctors may test some of your blood to see which group it belongs to.

The rhesus factor

Another system looks for a chemical called rhesus factor in the blood. Blood with the chemical is rhesus positive (Rh+). Blood that does not contain it is rhesus negative (Rh–).

The rhesus factor was first discovered in rhesus monkeys.

Q&A

What is a blood transfusion?

If you have a serious accident or an operation, you may lose a lot of blood. Doctors may use blood from a blood donor to replace the lost blood. This is called a blood transfusion. The blood groups of the patient and donor are tested so that the patient receives the matching blood type.

Rh– blood can be given to an Rh+ person. But Rh+ blood will make an Rh– person very ill. If an Rh+ mother is expecting an Rh– baby, her blood can harm the baby. The mother is given an injection to protect the baby.

ABO and rhesus blood groups are usually used together. For example, someone might say they are 'AB+'. This means their ABO group is AB and they are Rh+.

Giving **Blood**

Giving blood saves lives. Doctors need donated blood to replace any blood that might be lost during a major operation. People who have serious accidents may need blood transfusions to replace lost blood. Patients with some illnesses, such as leukaemia and anaemia, may also need donated blood.

Giving blood may help to save another person's life.

Blood donors

Different countries have different rules about who can give blood. Giving blood may harm you if your body is still growing. Some countries do not allow the elderly to give blood.

To give blood, people go to a blood donation centre. Before a person gives blood, they have to answer certain questions to make sure they are suitable. A small amount of blood is tested to make sure it is safe to go ahead.

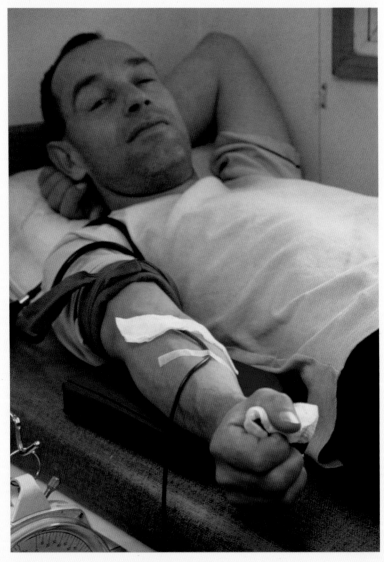

Taking blood

The donor sits or lies on a special chair or bed. A hollow

This large refrigerator is full of donated blood.

needle is put into a **vein** at the inside of their elbow. Blood flows through the needle, down a plastic tube and into a collecting bag. When the bag is full, the donor may rest a while.

Blood banks

Donated blood is refrigerated and stored in 'blood banks'. It is often separated into **red blood cells**, **white blood cells**, **platelets** and **plasma**. One blood donation may treat several people. For example, one patient may need plasma and another red blood cells.

Q&A

Is donated blood safe?

Donated blood is always tested to find out which group it belongs to. It is also tested for **viruses** or anything that may harm or pass on a disease to a patient. Scientists are constantly improving tests to check the donated blood is safe.

Blood Problems

Most people have healthy blood. However, some people have serious blood disorders.

Haemophilia

Haemophilia prevents the blood from clotting properly. This condition runs in families. People with haemophilia bruise easily. If they cut themselves it is very difficult to stop the bleeding. Haemophilia can be treated by regular injections of blood-clotting chemicals.

Sickle-cell anaemia

In this disease **red blood cells** become stretched and twisted. These red blood cells carry less **oxygen** than normal red blood cells. This means the person feels tired and weak. The cells may block blood vessels, causing pain. Sickle-cell anaemia can be treated by medicines and blood transfusions.

In sickle-cell anaemia, red blood cells become deformed and twisted.

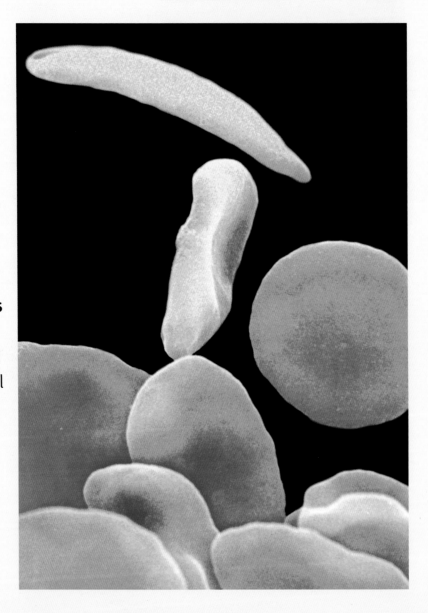

Sickle-cell anaemia is more common in countries around the equator. Malaria, a disease carried by mosquitoes, is also common there. Sickle cells make blood poisonous to these mosquitoes and protects against malaria!

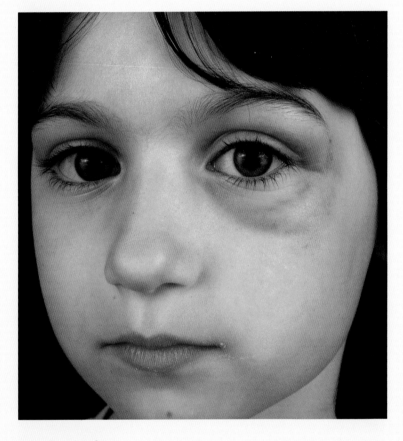

Bruises may hurt but they soon heal.

Leukaemia

Leukaemia makes the body produce too many **white blood cells,** which do not develop properly. This leaves the body open to infection. The extra white blood cells prevent the bone marrow from making red blood cells. The body cannot transport enough oxygen. This makes the person feel weak. Leukaemia is treated with special medicines and radiation. Some patients may receive a bone marrow transplant.

Q&A

What is a bruise?

When you bang your skin, blood vessels underneath may break and blood leaks out of them. The blood spreads under the skin, leaving a dark, purply-blue mark – a bruise. The colour fades as the body breaks up the blood cells and clears them away. After a few days, the bruise vanishes.

Glossary

aorta The main artery carrying blood away from the heart.

artery One of the large blood vessels carrying blood away from the heart.

atrium (plural: atria) One of the upper chambers of the heart.

capillary One of the tiniest blood vessels.

carbon dioxide A waste gas produced by the body.

cardiac To do with the heart.

circulation The movement of blood around the body.

coronary To do with the heart.

diaphragm A sheet of muscle below the lungs.

digestive system Organs that break up and absorb your food.

germs Micro-organisms that can cause illness.

kidneys Organs that remove waste salts and water from the blood.

liver The organ that controls many chemical reactions in the body.

nutrients The parts of your food that your body can use.

oxygen A gas that every part of your body needs in order to stay alive.

pericardium The outer covering of the heart.

plasma The liquid part of the blood.

platelet A tiny cell fragment that helps blood to clot.

pulmonary To do with the lungs.

red blood cell The part of the blood that carries oxygen.

ribcage Bones that form the chest and protect the heart and lungs.

septum The central wall separating the two sides of the heart.

valve A flap that controls the direction of blood flow.

vein The blood vessel that carries blood back to the heart.

vena cava (plural: venae cavae) The main vein that carries blood back to the heart.

ventricle One of the lower chambers of the heart.

virus A micro-organism that can cause illness.

white blood cell The part of the blood that protects you from illness and infection.

Further Information

Books

Body Science: The Heart in Action
by Richard Walker (Franklin Watts, 2004)
Kingfisher Knowledge: Human Body
by Richard Walker (Kingfisher, 2006)
My Healthy Body: Blood and Heart
by Jen Green (Franklin Watts, 2003)
Our Bodies: The Heart, Lungs and Blood
by Steve Parker (Wayland, 2003)
The Oxford Children's A to Z of the Human Body
by Bridget and Neil Ardley (Oxford University Press, 2003)
Usborne Internet-Linked Complete Book of the Human Body
by Anna Claybourne (Usborne Publishing, 2003)

Websites

www.fi.edu/learn/heart/

www.bbc.co.uk/science/humanbody/body/factfiles/heart/heart.shtml

kidshealth.org/kid/htbw/heart.html

Index

Page numbers in **bold** refer to illustrations.